Sea of Dust

Kevin Finn

Some poems contained herein were previously published in the chapbook *Exit Wounds* (Amsterdam Press), and the journals *Aethlon, Burning Bush II, Coal Hill Review, Plain Spoke,* and *Tiger's Eye Journal.*

SEA OF DUST

ISBN: 978-1-926616-56-8

Published by Six Gallery Press

Cover Photo by Martin Proll

Cover Design by Sean Finn

First Printing, December 2013

for JPF

Contents

The Meridians

Our world is slanted.

Like blacktop, it delivers
the tires, the corroded steel—

(the tempered metal).

I reach for a blackened sky,
come down like a white feather.

You reach   there
                    find me brittle,
cast   aside.

And now, the cat's rheumy eyes;
you let it out, seem awake in your sleep.

I am awake in my sleep!

Dreams take us to where the child
lies between us, slumbers.

We whimper—currents in our bodies, meridians.

What does the road hold for us?

The curl of grass?

We hope for bright light, a rich sun
to move through curtains,

blankets across our legs—

my hands are like that,
like lightning rods—

it's simple to become anything.

I watch as the magnets touch your shoulder,
wake her and caress her temples.

Sometimes, a sparrow will crush
the seed you put out for it, sometimes

the squirrel, a thief, gorges,
and nothing is left.

In my mind, I have the spark of gears.
I shut your eyes, a slight touch of my hand:

it has just begun to shine through.

America

We're talking about the moon,
the changes in us, the changes in you.

And we were listening to the clang,
the deep resonance of the gong—

it was deafening, it was ecstatic listening.

We walked down the moonlit road
deep into summer. Past the houses,

past the raw, bitter smell of the flowering trees.
How could we ever depart from that one

thing, that source of things? We saw a house,
the door stripped from its hinges,

like a decaying dream of freedom. Lank,
bone-thin, kept awake in its starry night.

We passed its leaning frame.

Crossroads at Three Forks

The thresher grinds Crustacean bones.

The summer rain falls,
and the words of a priest:

> *Is it you who breaks*
> *His sword, straw like*
> *needles, across my back?*

> Or,

> *He is an oracle of plenty,*
> *a cornucopia of kale,*
> *blessed tomato, mud-caked beets!*

I'll cast the first stone in the air—
let it hit me, my head in vice, my heart

in the gutter. 'Til I take off my skin,
and hear the rooster crow, crow, crow.

Coyote

A dead hare.

I kneel to groom what's
left of the matted fur.

Scavengers, we worship
our own gods.

We tremble in each
other's presence.

The Crow

I look out over tall grass,
and know its name:

black wings, black throat
black eyes. I can't stand

to hear its song, the sound
of rust and cut metal,

the sound of useful trash.

I'm close to the ground,
bathe in a stream that runs

over orange mine runoff.

You came up here from Helena
to die, two cases of beer, a bottle

of Old Crow. You swear at
black brown seedpods, curse

them as writhing snakes.
Take a stick to 'em, then

turn over and fold your black wings.

The Indigenous Hour

Is it easy to forget
 the reasons why?

Even as the thud of drums

  drew songs from you, songs

that worked from your gut out
     into the purple

grit of desert,
    the world sped on.

And, as time coalesced,

    when your body retreated

into breath and song...

      Nothing's easy, is it?

Your soul, a comet on fire,

its descent wild and captive in a universal
          ellipsis,

then let go into the stark whiteness

        of hospital bed linens.

Fear takes on many forms—
     the stagnant fear turns to shadow.

We too were once wild, fearless.
                    We too were once of this earth.

We're removing ourselves hour by hour.
                    These things you sometimes
forget.

Just don't forget.

The Collection

The mountain is worthless,
save its beauty, curtained by clouds.

It waits, like I do, my pockets free
of change. I lie on the grass, look

at the sky, it's worthless.

I enjoy this game.

Wild flowers wake the foothills:
blue lavender, white clover,

tiny bees alive and working.

You sit in the church pew
with the others, help take up

the collection.

At the end, you walk out
of glass doors, your holiness

renewed, the weight of the week
heavy around your eyes, the creases

in your forehead burrow into age.

Paul

He'd sleep during the day—

      a canvas army tent on
      the high plains of summer.

We talked of Christ's sword,
      felt the wind blow like prophecy:
maybe justice, maybe love.

Through the mossy rocks, we
      crossed the narrow elk trails
      somewhere east of Gardner.

We drank cheap beer,

      I strummed my guitar,
      sang songs, sang "oh, life

      is but a dream!"

I left him there,
bound for the Willamette,
      his long stringy hair
soaked with sweat
at the nape of his neck.

Lost City, Montana

She wore red lipstick.

It seemed uneven,

how it circled the lips.

She kept a knife

strapped to her thigh,

showed me the weapon
in the heat.

She collected air
from outside,
brought it inside
to me,
into a red tent she shared

with the boy she found

along the way.

When we ran out
             of wilderness,

the greyhound carried us out,

carried us to San Francisco,

      where strip clubs build and condense

on Broadway, where the heart speeds up,

            and the city quiets it,

where the lost city is like a daydream in the grainy

afterlife of a butcher's placid cleaving.

Badlands

Levels of equation,
academic utterances,

fuck in a clandestine fortress.

A chandelier hangs
from walls of oak;

shields its light
from a cavalcade

of wild horses.

Outside the Walls

Every time the brain
fires true revelation,

it misfires like
a cooling barrel.

When you showed up,
they weren't sure

if you had made up
the part about who you were.

It might've been easier
to carry your thin book

of poems, like a modern Bible,
down the aisle, and out

the engraved glass doors
of the church, and leave it

among the ferns,

and let the trees serve
as church walls, just to sit,

and breathe, and wait.

You and grief were close.

Your closeness wavered
in candlelight and stood

still—a sparrow hidden
among the oak.

Something stirred between
you and God.

It was the pen, the paper—
            an exclamation!

It was at last spirit, not originating,
but borrowing the future.

Crow Feather's Baby

She's gone, cramped in—cut right out,
        crow-feathered hair blown back, back

from her brow, rainsoaked. She sleeps
                under pine, blue needles, a
blanket of light built inside
                  itself. The cold of farewell
carries her out, leaves me here.

She's peeled back, like old skin,
        a test to love,   *Try*, she said,
stumble, lose yourself, this time.
Pose yourself inside and out,
      inside and out, inside and out.

The Wisdom Letters

The naked body, its breast heaved
and then, the mewing of the lamb.

When she moves—a great stasis relieved.

When she breathes, so does the lance
of sovereignty: the great death.

And I'm given a song,

> *The song of the ocean,*
> *the song of the sea,*
> *the breath of salt*
> *the blue skin breathes.*

As the muse sounds itself—a banshee
in a sea of machines, it cuts through
                          and disappears

beyond a wall of sound.

Apple and the Light

I take the night and spill the light into it.
I let the light shine on you,

smear the blood of all sorrow on your brow.

Let the judge speak.

Some nights I take the light of day,
let it spill onto you, let your hair spill

onto your naked shoulders.

Now is the time of letting go.
Letting go of what you've come to expect,

the directions you've taken.

The ruthless snow beats at your weakened skin—
your quarters the snow beaten mountain.

Truth beats at your weakened heart,
    How it beats, so!

I've taken from you a request, let the light spill
into the corners of your room, let the naked body rest.

I give to you what I've returned, bought back, sold
and wrapped in white paper.

A word to love, a word

                            to take.

Let the light spill into your eyes and let it spill
into your reckless course.

Let the judge speak.

Let the light of morning beckon you home.

Let it touch your reckless heart, let the snow drive
you to me.

Let the shudder of light pierce your wooden side.
Let your image fall.

I'll give you words to love; a walk in distant canyons.
I'll give you wild flowers.

Free Will

The thunderous ricochet of death
reported and reinvented with each

strapped dollar,

we wait while you sip tonight's

first beer, after you wash the hundred

thousand year old sawdust off of
yesterday's boots.

Days go by, and we find we're not
so different.

We trade our lies for wild meat.

We pretend we live the lives we wanted.

This is what makes us wake up in the morning
in a world without end.

The sun rises, then the moon.

The door opens, then shuts.

All opportunity is a variant of one choice.

All beings hold one finger up,
not to belittle, but to define.

Given the options, you shy away from
choice,

run to the profiteers and their armies.

Say it wasn't you!

Say your bloodied hands are not your own!

But then, given our options, nothing
is justified more than this.

The Great Death

My hands have given
nothing to the world, but song.

Where once there was water—
now a sea of dust.

Void

The water dragon
                blue and dank
to snuff it,
                  I'll call the emptiness

of Nirvana something;
                      a serpent's
tongue, a coiled rope.

Time has elapsed
                but not ended.

A vessel prompted
                to silence: memory.

You bathe with stone,
                the river to cleanse you.

'Til the sound of the bell
                (when there's nothing).

Study in Black and White

Black water pushes against
the wooden dock

the wood sleeps like the black moon.

I shed my clothes, quietly part

the water, follow your white shape,
work my way to you.

You swim in bare skin;
push ripples into the lake—

the drone of cricket song
alive in the night.

Sun Koan

These are black days,
              she says, and I
eat burning coals, breathe fire.

This is how it is when we kiss:

(hand, mouth, breath,
             hips, breast, lips).

And sometimes, the sun burns
        through our windows.

It's inside the room, fragmented
        and broken.

Shards of black metallic light pinch

and close her eyes, blue within blue,
like a manta ray passing a school.

The water, clear, parts to the long assassin.

We're
        in the center, then, we're tentacles.

We find we are the answer—
this closeness, this need to know.

The tall conical spruce,
the very cut of the blade,

the discarded husk of the blade,
        the last moment,

It's all here, feel?
Yes I can feel it,
it departs,
it departs.

Dragonflies

My eyes blink,
each frame
lit by sun
      —dragonflies—

(neon blue, neon green);

a pair of wings amid metallic
silver fish.
               A concrete pipe,
               wide mouth open,

chokes water into a pool.

You wade in up to your knees,
with shoes made of discarded tires;

      your yellow print dress pulled
up to your thighs.

Grass cuts through
asphalt over head—

you walk in the shallow water
and make the perfect reflection:

      a survivor, something human.

Prism of Memory

I'm taking apart memories.
Each photo a fragment of memory.

Each is precious and causal.
How can I break the chain

of events, take out the bad
parts, the parts that bind?

You look younger now
than you did that first time

we exhaled deep,
passed it back and forth

until I snuffed it in the clean earth.

The light filters into the room

through a prism, a dangling
crystal, a rainbow made of mineral.

Just quiet light, chance color,
perfect symmetry.

Hope for a Sound Birth

It's thirty-seven weeks
into your pregnancy.

I have a dream
we're building a river.

We're building a birth canal
with little pennies for tools.

It's hard to work the land
with little pennies.

Maybe we should use real tools.
But right now, all we have are pennies.

I'm a mile up the road where the river
starts and the land widens.

We build the river and slide down it
with hands tied to ropes on the sides of rafts.

Above you, the moon is fully eclipsed.

Portal of White Oak

We walked past the grove
we knew by name.

It was a sacred sound,
it sounded as if an owl

flew out of the twilight.

I remember the summer,
the infinite light.

You wore a red print
dress, a straw hat.

You would hold my hand,
the child in the sandbox,

the ruins of the old house,
the brick and crusted mortar.

We walked past the grove,
the fringe of silent oak,

the yellow-tongued iris.

The light lingered.
The sun shone through

the door. Then, the moon
reflected, an arabesque.

If this Poem were a Haiku

I'd see in the well, fetch water
for the dry, cracked earth.

Time stops when you walk
in the door.

You are sweet to taste, soft
like cured leather to touch.

If I could, I'd fashion you myself
with my bare hands.

Little, thin, hollow bones,
        (the wings of the dove),

the petals of the iris,

the smooth scales of the piano.

I'd wake to the sound of the brush.

Chalk white bristles—

the morning open to bird song.

A far away breathing organ,
        (lips of the flutist).

We're cut adrift, the wish
of emergence, the clear bloodlines

of a mountain stream.

The Arboretum

I walked the woods—
traces of sunlight, small animals,

horse hooves. My prints
on the rainsoaked earth.

I found feathers—
dreams of meadows
in the dark arboretum.

One of the doors stayed
open and still the rain fell.

I used a hammer to nail up
a picture of a Native Christ.

Then, put feathers behind it,
hawk and grouse.

I went in, and shut the door
        to light, to shadow,
to dream, again.

Reflection

You have to be faster

                  than the shadow beside you,
than the boy who gazes
                  at the shadow before you,
than the secret death of the boy

who knows.

You have to be as the people who walk beside you,
                                reflective as rain.

The sacred path of life, of all life, alters and directs us

to make barren the light-led path,

but darker the path of ignorance, to part decision like wind.

And from the north she comes, she clings to you, a beast

primitive, feral, still of the earth.

She clings and parts your hair.

She smells of lavender, wood smoke, truth and heart.

She is the unseen, the wild horses who gather
as the rain moves in, as the sun moves; as clouds.

You can almost see.

You can almost feel the quickening of heaven.

The Hollow

Take the road, the old cobblestones,
                   into the trees' living shadows,
into
                   the darkest night.

It's here you'll see the faint glint of steel,
                 the bridge spans above you like
a calling into her arms, her arms (the channel of peace).

          Somewhere, missiles break apart love's own echo:
the passionate light of war.

You crawled out, home, to the money stored there, under
                         the graffiti

that seemed to grow out of the concrete sheet.
                 You pulled the concrete onto you.
The tree-lined canopy of asphalt.

Then, to drink again at the lake's edge.

               I've never slept so soundly.

The wheels above you, headlights reach into night, pull
     at it; cross the bridge.

Once, a man shook himself loose from the tether
that held him to her wrist.

Now, the ash white sky.

Now, the morning dew, the breaking point

                 of the last wilderness.

Divinity

They were right.

I did ride the moon

     well into the night,

held antlers

     planted on my head.

I knew the spirit's

     descent as the falcon

to field mouse,

     as the meteor to earth.

I cursed the monument—

     a great stone phallus

piercing the night sky.

And all along, disguised

       in golden skin—

a trench, a war head.

Western Psychiatric Elopement Risk

It's morning, and I put down
the paper. I'm told to shower,

so I do, use baby shampoo
to wash my hair and body.

Tepid water touches the tiled surface,
leaks out of the concealing

shower curtain and onto the
bathroom floor.

I use a towel to dry my feet,
wipe the face of the mirror,

I look into the glass, see my
reflection, try not to notice

Palestine is in ruins.

The east wing is closed off now
to control *elopement,* a word

like *fleeing*, a word
common as armies

marching into cities—concrete
slabs. It's summer and

I can't sleep for the falling.

Violins

He stands before the machine of war—
a house of fire, the road is on fire.

The tendency of smoke to rise,
or carry itself on the wind.

The act itself outlawed.

Here, the only recourse is the timpani,

or the slow diminish of violins.

There's no time for gentler things—
where love is, where the family gathers to eat.

He blossoms like a lily.

DMZ

The crane captures fish,
           a chime, an echo.

She lives in this place.

She passes freely from north
           to south, to roost
to create
           the next gliding generation.

Somewhere stands peace.

I'm sipping champagne
           in the year of the tiger,

wooden, green—
           a bamboo shoot in water,

or the flowering monarch,
           the pitch of wind, soft to the ear.

Khyber Pass

A locust grants us farewell,
     O, Summer!
     O, Bye-bye.

And the spider in the cedar tree:
     Today, I walked with a clamorous gait.
     Today, I spun a web.
     Today, I found my prey.

Somewhere I lay the revolver down.

Beside me a dog sleeps.

Somewhere a lion tears the flesh off
its prey.

Somewhere we are sleeping.

Somewhere stands the pass in the mountains.

Let's break bread tonight,

eat out of the same bowl
as the ones who've conjured us,

with a brush of sand, a wave of power.

If Only a New Day

I've seen hundreds of suns rising, the moon
in the night, and I've seen the heads torn

from the torso, the powdery afterglow
of bombs lit by such force, we all wake

feeling the shock. I'm underground

in the fibrous intestines of the nation's
insides, its guts, its desires.

You've seen how dreams make you see
yourself, everything mirroring the omens

in your head. Think back a little further,
green rock, owl feather, Egyptian sky—

these dreams are minor, some spirit to take hold—
you're going to find just what you needed,

shed the old leathery skin, and beat the flesh
until it's supple, pliable, edible, then go.

Nuclear

The dark, steel drums of waste
sink beneath the mountain.

The hot circuitry moans—
power lines feed the things

(that wash over me).

A crowd draws in, closer
to a vast desert.

A crowd collapses:
sinkholes—into fathoms
                        of what we want.

Tell me of the arctic hare, the caribou.

How silver and gold cities return to dust.

Offshore

I wanted a ring, a carved Indian
                 face, or a horsehair instrument

that droned, but the Gulf was beaten

with oil in its gills and feathers—

a desperate mix, viscous and black.

Give me the horse skull,

keep the credit card.

Give me a great blue adventure,

               I'll just stand and stare.

      The pelican grounded,
      the sand like cement,
      the open wound of our planet
      cauterized just enough.

The shallow drill headed for bone.

The Dolphins

Days have passed.
> And I wonder what I've missed.

They've gone to the deep,
> to the endless horizon of sea.

The black fins raised just
> above the breaking waves—

the brackish foam white
> against the night.

I still feel it—the lasso of current.
> How the sea moves below me—

the itinerant looking for the right
> word for welcome.

Spirits

Of the earth,

        I hold the broken cup.

Being human,
           I walk the beach,

see ruin, the hand of myriad spirits.

           I hold flowers out to give.

The prayers are quick, a feint light, here.

           I'm shielded by dark robes,
              an effigy

of reason weighted by emptiness.

The pull of gravity—a wave pulling

           lives towards parallels—universe,

             planet, its people.

Theirs is the reactor, the lost.

Voice

If this is the holy desert, I'd host gods—

like the vanished lion, the caterwaul.

If I were a poet, I'd plant this tree,

and, later, maybe a word would fall,

maybe an apple would fall: just

the word, *wisdom.*

Of loss, the diminished fire—
but then, nothing outlives love,

and choice, is choice; the touched—
                                    touched.

Revolve the door and become.

Kata

I've come to welcome form,
to bring the body to spirit.

To let in light, as the mind knows,

to push forward, step back and—block,
foot set in motion, leg chambered quickly.

And the last, hands.

Budo

As it begins—a stone

        set in water, ripples pulled

to the center, to the edges
          of the body.

And, as the light is shrouded then to black,

a dwelling place also within, and there,
a longer road, still.

And we see the dwarfed
arbor, the clear visage

of mountains—the soft footing of its dwelling.

To be as it begins, stone set in water, ripples pulled
to the edge of the body (may the body know it!),

to speak of it, to act.

Kiai

The blood of his father's father's father:
a shrine awaits its spirits. An ancestral

doorway, a diver parts the water to seek
its hidden pearls.

Is it the sound a chain makes as it breaks
the bamboo from its stalk? Or, is it

the sound of new breath, the sound a

newborn makes as it wakes
to this world for the first time?

I'll make a disembodied vowel.

I'll make a disembodied syllable
for peace. And I'll battle in my own dreams

for it, I dream in my own waking moment
for it. Some kind of sane waking,

  Let us know it in this life!

And so, a great undertaking:
a life once lived driven out,

while time projects *tradition*,
a spirit breath, a breath of life.

The Fishing Crane

What do you know
that you know nothing of?

A seamless invisibility—
the crooked branches, the exposed roots.

Tell of it then, tell of it and remain.
Then, train the body, work precision:

the white lily, the folded moon flower,
the waxing moon.

The seed is ripe, it breaks the earth,
thirsts for rain.

I've washed the blood from my brow.
Look from the mountain.

The mists cover my face.
I give little flashes of light from a mirror—

the eye blinks, reflects it back (the light).
Tell of it. Tell the breath of it, the remainder,

the fool's understanding.
Give me sand through my fingers,

I'll try to hold on.
Now, one step from the door,

a thousand steps towards the beginning,
the sight of carrion; the fishing crane.

At the Edge of the Ohio

The ribcage protrudes.

There's a remnant of fur.

The road's stained red.

Did the creature hear death

                        before the impact?

Or, was its cry lost on

                       the hollow sound of cars—

a monstrous tour de force

                       against the interstate.

Some believe intelligence reigns

in a land besieged by Sequoia, Sundance.

Did you see it coming?

Once I had a dream.

The sky had opened,

the sun shone, as clouds

reflected and the river

                       was parted by land.

I heard voices from the clouds,
                              but didn't know the way,

didn't know the way to row—

to find current to land.

Zoo

The gorilla peeled its banana,
sat in the dusty yard. The passing

crowd stared at the beast.

I left mid-day, walked up the
ramp and through the lot,

past Negley and into the trees.

I smoked a cigarette.

The sun sank.
I pressed on.

I craned my neck.
The drains poured into the river.

Is there anything good left in me?

The flight of the songbird—
the ATM at Baum,

the resilient sparrow.

I think of Francis, who bore

wild beasts as brothers, who
knew them: family.

Then, the smog lifted, cut out
of forged steel the lifeless lot

of the city.

Didn't it look beautiful as the sun

set over it that day?

I'm building an ark out of river currents.
I'm preaching the songs of the rivers.

The chorus out of sight,
as a barge breaks the water.

Somewhere the black body finds
its way to the scrap yard, to its rusty shore.

I lift one foot before the other, take
the undertaking.

Made in the USA
Charleston, SC
26 June 2014